Weirdibeasts

Weird Spooky Day

There are lots of Early Reader stories you might enjoy.

Look at the back of the book or, for a complete list, visit www.orionchildrensbooks.co.uk

Weirdibeasts

Weird Spooky Day

By Alan, Rachel
and Megan Gibbons

Illustrated by
Jane Porter

Orion
Children's Books

ORION CHILDREN'S BOOKS

First published in Great Britain in 2016
by Hodder and Stoughton

1 3 5 7 9 10 8 6 4 2

A CIP catalogue record for this book
is available from the British Library.

ISBN 978 1 4440 1282 8

Printed and bound in China

The paper and board used in this book are from well-managed
forests and other responsible sources.

Orion Children's Books
An imprint of
Hachette Children's Group
Part of Hodder and Stoughton
Carmelite House
50 Victoria Embankment
London EC4Y 0DZ

An Hachette UK Company
www.hachette.co.uk

www.orionchildrensbooks.co.uk

To the Hillsborough families

Contents

One

Halloween was coming. But not just any Halloween — it was a Weirdibeasts' Halloween.

It all began when Mrs Creature, the Weirdibeasts' teacher, handed out a pile of invitations.

**ARE YOU SCARED OF THE DARK?
DO YOU JUMP WHEN THINGS
GO BUMP IN THE NIGHT?
DON'T MISS THE ANIMAL
TOWN HALLOWEEN PARTY!**

Food and Games
A special prize for the best fancy dress
This Saturday
Town Hall
8pm

"A party!" Katie Cat squealed. "I love parties."
"Me too," barked Dabby Dog.
"I like dressing up."
He wagged his tail.

Now Dabby wasn't just any little dog – he was a Hedgehound. All his spikes stood on end.
"Ouch!" grunted Penny Pig. "That prickles."

"That's nothing," said Ricky Rabbit. "What about your big, fluffy squirrel tail? That tickles!"

The Weirdibeasts were quite a mixed up bunch. Soon they were all barking and neighing, hooting and snorting as they talked about what they were going to wear. They all imagined their costumes. "Cool," Tony said.

"This is going to be great," Katie giggled.

"So scary!" Penny chuckled.

"I'm sure to win," Ricky Rabbit said.

"Well, I'm going to be a
postman," Dabby Dog told them.
Everybody turned and looked.
"A postman?" Katie Cat said.
"That's not scary."

"It is," Dabby said. "He pushes letters through my door. Once one landed right on my nose."

The other Weirdibeasts shook
their heads.

Two

That Saturday morning, Katie Cat and her mum went to the fancy dress shop.

The rest of the Weirdibeasts were already there.

"Look," Tony said, "I'm going to be the meanest burglar ever. Look at my swag bag."

"That's nothing," Katie said.
"Look at my broom and my
pointy hat."

"I'm going to beat every one of you," Penny Pig said. "Look at these scary vampire teeth."

"Oh no, you won't," Ricky
Rabbit said, holding up a roll of
bandages. "Ricky the monster
mummy will terrify everybody."
He held out his claws scarily.
The Weirdibeasts squealed and
ran away laughing as he plodded
after them.

"My costume is easily the best,"
Dabby Dog said. "Look at my
scary postman's bag."

"You can't go as a postman!" the other Weirdibeasts cried. "That's silly."

"You're silly," he sulked, clutching his postman's bag in a huff.

They took their costumes to the counter to pay. There was no time to try them on.

Three

But when Katie Cat got home
there was a problem.
A big one.
The costume wouldn't go on!

"Mum!" she twit-twooed. "It won't fit."

"Your wings are the problem,"
Mum said. "Witches don't have
wings. That's why they have
broomsticks."
Katie was so upset.

Just then there was a knock at
the door. It was Penny Pig.
"My tail keeps sticking out of my
cape. I don't look like a vampire
at all."

Tony Pony was next to arrive.
"My striped jumper won't go
over my wings."

Katie nodded.
"Just like me," she said sadly.

Things were no better when Ricky Rabbit turned up. "My claws keep cutting my bandages," he wailed. "I'm a mess!"

Dabby Dog was last to arrive,
looking very pleased with himself.
"Boo!" he barked. "I'm the
scariest postman ever."
"Postmen aren't scary!" the other
Weirdibeasts shouted.

"Well, I'm scared of them,"
Dabby woofed.

Katie Cat's mum listened to all the terrible muttering and moaning and grunting and groaning.

"I have an idea," she said. Then she pulled some white sheets out of the washing.

Four

By the time the Weirdibeasts got to the Town Hall, all the other animals were there.

The Weirdibeasts peeked through the window and looked at all the fantastic costumes.

There were dragons and
monsters, zombies and
werewolves, walking pumpkins
and beastly bats.

"They're all so good," sighed Tony Pony.
"They're brilliant," groaned Ricky Rabbit.
"They're so much better than us," said Penny Pig.

"Well none of them are as good as me," said Dabby Dog, putting his postman's hat on his head and strutting through the door proudly.

Ellie Mouse was already there. "I don't believe it!" Katie Cat said, staring at the mouse-sized elephant. "She's come as a ghost, just like us."

Of course, Ellie didn't need
a sheet to cover her. A
handkerchief was quite big
enough.

"We can't go in looking like this," Katie Cat said. "Everybody else looks better than us, even Dabby Dog."

Through the window, they could
see everybody crowding round
Dabby Dog, asking about his
costume.

"Well, I'm taking this stupid sheet off," Ricky Rabbit said. "Me too," Penny Pig said. "'I agree," Tony Pony neighed. "I'd rather go just as I am."

The Weirdibeasts were so fed up.
Everything had gone wrong.

They took a deep breath and
sneaked into the fancy dress party.

Suddenly, it went silent. All they could hear were gasps from the other animals.

"Look," one said.

"Wow!" said another.

"Those wings look so real."

"A cat that's an owl."

"A pony that's an eagle."

Everybody was staring at the
Miaowl and the Ponyeagle, the
Crabbit and the Piggel.

Ellie took off her sheet and
everybody clapped.

"How did they do it?" the crowd gasped.

The judge, Mayor Moose,
walked to the microphone.
"In joint second place," he said.
"The Weirdibeasts!"

"Second?" Katie Cat twit-twooed. "So who's first?"

"And in first place," Mayor Moose said. "Can I have a drum roll? The scariest postman ever ... Dabby Dog!"

Dabby Dog went to get his
prize. He winked at his friends.
"Told you," he barked.

"This," Katie Cat said, "is the weirdest Halloween ever."

What are you going to read next?

Don't miss the other adventures in the **Weirdibeasts** series . . .

Join Katie Cat on her first day at school in **Weird School Day**.

Race with the Weirdibeasts in **Weird Sports Day**.

For more Halloween fun,
read all about
The Witch Dog,

Early Reader

THE Witch Dog

By Margaret Mahy
Illustrated by Sam Usher

or learn how to grow
pumpkins with
Lottie and Dottie.

Early Reader

Lottie and Dottie
Grow Pumpkins

Claire Burgess
Illustrated by Marijke van Veldhoven